Tao of Trading

An Illustrative Guide in Understanding the Psychology of the Stock Market

J.M. Benavidez Estoque

Illustrated by Lyndon M. Regalario

Published by Book of Life Publishing

For permissions, inquiries, or correspondence, contact:
estoque0818@yahoo.com

Table of Contents

Introduction

Ka-ching! It's payday again. After budgeting all of your expenses for the month, you realized that you have some extra cash left. In your head, you asked yourself where you would spend this extra money?

Buy new gadgets? Nope. You have one already. There is no need for another one. Hmmm... How about a new pair of shoes or a new set of clothes? But then you realized that you haven't used the other ones that you've recently bought either.

Then you thought, "How about this time, I should try to invest this money and let it grow?" and at that very moment, two words began to flash in your head... STOCK MARKET.

This book is written for you who are thinking of investing in the Stock Market but don't know how it works and for those who had already started investing and trading but STILL do not have any idea what is going through but be gullible enough on fake news and fake Stock Market Gurus and blindly follow Technical Indicators and Charts but are clueless what on earth is going on?

CAVEAT EMPTOR. If you believe this book will make you easily rich just by reading this book, better not proceed with reading. But by learning the principles laid down by the author of this book as observed on his active days in the Stock Market, you too, with practice and continuous learning, can grasp this foreign battlefield and eventually make decisions on your own as to when and what stocks are ripe for buying and as to when and what stocks are ripe for selling for profit!

Many people are dreaming of exploring the world of the Stock Market, but do not tread the path that leads to it because of fear. They felt it to be an unknown world, and perhaps after even starting, because of a lack of understanding of how it works, they immediately gave up and thought that it is not for them.

I, too, my friend, started in the Stock Market without knowing anything at first. I am just a simple person who does not have degrees in Economics, Business Management, or any related courses. But then, I realized that your degree does not matter. For as long as you understand the basic principles underlying it and know how it works, you can invest and make money in the Stock Market.

You don't need to complicate yourself with all these technicalities and mumbo-jumbo stuff. As long as you grasp what is essential, then you are already good to go. Perhaps armed with the basic but strong foundations, you can even beat those who equip themselves of many technical terms and many technical charts which they themselves do not understand the real essence of what they are doing.

This book is written by a simple person like you. You can expect that it will be written in simple words that you yourself can easily understand, plus a helpful illustration that can help you grasp the concept through its creative metaphors.

A French philosopher and writer once said, “What is essential is invisible to the eye”.

People often complicate their brains by immersing in the technicalities, which in the end, they lose themselves in the process. That most of the, you only had to understand its essence, its core simple concept.

This book will not teach you technical analysis but the underlying principles that govern them. It will not confuse nor intimidate you with charts nor with scary terminologies, but rather on how the Stock Market works and just on how it is purely driven by the Buyers and the Sellers who are also people like you. And when we speak of people, we are speaking of the majority (if not all) who are also driven by their emotions rather than their reason. People are more irrational than they think they are rational.

Once you enter the world of the Stock Market armed with the principles and observations as laid down by this book, what you will now see behind that screen of intimidating charts, graphs, and digits are those people behind the majority being driven by emotions of greed and fear.

This is how the Stock Market works. The Stock Market is 80% a game of psychology.

What is the Stock Market

Imagine a publicly listed company is a pizza— a big big pizza! This pizza is divided into many slices. The ownership of a company is divided into many "stocks" or "shares". People who own stocks or shares of a company are called "shareholders". Nowadays, people do not need any more to have a 1 million worth of money on their bank account just to purchase stocks or shares of ownership from a company.

You can buy or sell your stock or shares at whatever price you would like. You can offer to buy someone's share at a lower or higher price. You can offer to sell your share at a lower or higher price, too. Of course, what you want and what you need is to buy someone's share at a lower price and sell it later at a higher price in order to gain profits. But in reality, the opposite happens for many.

People can buy and sell stocks through a representative on the Stock Market. These representatives are called stockbrokers. Stock Brokers are those individuals and firms licensed and authorized by the government to handle transactions between a Buyer and a Seller. Most Buy and Sell transactions nowadays are already done online.

Stock Market Exchange is a venue where buyers and sellers meet, as represented by Stock Brokers, to transact the exchange of ownership of stocks or shares.

The basic forms of strategy in dealing withthe Stock Market are (1) Investing and (2) Trading.

Investing in the Stock Market is like putting a seed in carefully selected soil, hoping that after a long period of time, it will grow into a mature tree. As the seed matures into a tree, its value and its price also increase.

As some trees bear fruit as long as you don't chop them and sell their wood, some companies offer dividends as long as you don't sell your shares.

Trading in the Stock Market is like a buy-and-sell business. You just buy a particular stock at a cheap price from someone who wants to dispose of it and sell it at a higher price to someone willing to buy it.

Investing is a commitment, a long-term relationship. Trading is a fling, a short-term plan. However, due to careless study of a stock and lack of understanding of the Stock Market, a short-term plan becomes a long-term relationship and a long-term relationship becomes a short-term plan, which eventually leads to losses.

There are two ways to earn money in the Stock Market: (1) through Capital Appreciation and (2) through Dividends.

Capital Appreciation is when you buy a stock at a lower price and sell it at a higher price. Thus, your original capital, which you used to buy a stock, increased as you sold it at a higher price. For simple illustration: For example, you buy 1 share of stock ABC for P1.00. Later on, you sold it for P1.50. From your original P1.00, it increased to P1.50. Your capital, therefore, increased in value and therefore it appreciates.

Dividends are what the company gives to its shareholders as part of their share of the earnings of the company.

Now that we are introduced as to what basically is a Stock Market, let us now proceed to the underlying principles that govern the Stock Market.

The Tao of Trading *with Illustrations*

CHAPTER I:
The Psychology of the Market

Chapter I: The Psychology of the Market

The market is composed of two opposite forces

14

The Buyers

15

and The Sellers

The Buyers represent the
Demand

17

The Sellers represent the Supply

18

When the demand is high,
price tends to move up;

19

When the supply is high,
price tends move down.

20

The more buyers over the sellers,
the more the price moves up;

21

The more the sellers over the buyers,
the more the price moves down.

22

Price always follows three specific direction or trends:

23

Uptrend - Price can move up,
when there are more buyers than the sellers;

24

Uptrend - Price can move up,
when there are more buyers than the sellers;

24

Downtrend - Price can move down, when there are more sellers than the buyers;

25

No trend - Price moves sideways, when buyers and sellers both agree at a specific price range.

26

Reversal usually happens in an uptrend, when there are already about no more buyers but sellers;

27

Reversal usually happens in a downtrend, when there are already about no more sellers but buyers.

28

Always remember that in a market, the buyers are potential sellers in the future.

29

A buyer will already become a seller once he already assumed that the price had reached a point that it is already high enough to close a trading position and gain profits.

30

A new buyer will come-in once he already assumed that the price had reached a point that it is already low enough to open a trading position which could in turn provide them profits in the future.

31

Different buyers had each different criteria when a specific price is low enough to open a trading position

32

Different sellers had each different criteria when a specific price is high enough to close a trading position

33

When majority of the buyers agree that the specific price point is low enough to open a trading position, this specific point becomes the "support"

34

When majority of the sellers agree that the specific price point is high enough to close a trading position, this specific point becomes the "resistance"

35

A specific point becomes the "support", when it blocks and supports the price from moving down lower

36

A specific point becomes the "resistance", when it blocks and resists the price from moving up higher

37

Thus the price bounces back once it hits the support and the resistance

38

The price breaks the support when the sellers overcome the buyers and the majority of the buyers found a new lower price point that is cheaper enough to open a trading position

The price breaks the resistance when the buyers overcome the sellers and the majority of the sellers found a new higher price point that is more expensive (and more profitable) enough to close a trading position

A point of support, once broken,
may become the new resistance

41

A point of resistance, once broken, may become the new support.

42

Chapter II: The Trader

Section 1: The Nature of a Trader
Section 2: Accumulators and Distributors
Section 3: Gamblers
Section 4: When a Trader Buys and Sells
Section 5: Two Sentiments in Trading
Section 6: The Bulls and the Bears
Section 7: The Optimists and the Pessimists
Section 8: Two Dangerous Emotions in Trading
Section 9: The Psychology of Greed and Fear
Section 10: Heavy Buying and Heavy Selling
Section 11: Disasters in Trading
Section 12: Contrarian Trading Strategy

A trader is neither a buyer nor a seller

46

But encompasses both being both
a buyer and a seller

47

A person who only buys is not a trader,
but an accumulator unless he sells

48

A person who only sells is not a trader,
but a distributor unless he buys

49

A trader is a person who buy and sell for profit.
Otherwise he is not a trader.

50

A person who carelessly buy and sell is not a trader, but a gambler.

51

A good trader only buys when there is a good opportunity to buy

52

A good trader only sells when there is a good opportunity to sell

53

Thus created two divisions of trader in a market according to their sentiments

54

A trader who wishes and hopes for the price to rise up further is a "Bull"

55

A trader who wishes and hopes for the price to go down further is a "Bear"

56

A bull is a predator that strikes its prey upwards

57

A bear is a predator that drags its prey downwards

58

The Bulls are usually those who are waiting for the price to rise up until given an opportunity to sell at a higher price

The Bears are those who are waiting for the price to decline until given an opportunity to buy at a lower price

60

Market situation creates two divisions of traders according to their attitude

61

A trader becomes an optimist
when he gives more value to a commodity
than its actual value;

62

A trader becomes a pessimist
when he gives lesser value to a commodity
than its actual value

63

Pessimist

Optimist

Thus, a good trader takes profits through buying from a pessimist and selling to the optimist.

64

A good trader always keep himself in check from being vulnerable to two dangerous emotions in trading

65

one is when he is
GREEDY

66

the other one is when he is
FEARFUL

67

Emotions clouds the judgment of a trader

68

A trader may overestimate too much a commodity when he is greedy

69

A trader may underestimate too much a commodity when he is fearful

70

A greedy trader who buys would therefore pay even at a higher price believing that the price would even ascend higher soon

71

A fearful trader who buys would therefore not pay even at a lower price believing that the price would even descend lower soon

72

A greedy trader is therefore eager to buy to get in a trading position

73

While a fearful trader is therefore eager
to sell to get out a trading position

74

A greedy trader is overwhelmed by the desire of entering or staying in a trading position as soon as possible for the fear of being left-out on a current good price direction

75

THEIR EXPECTATION:

A fearful trader is overwhelmed by the desire of exiting or staying out of a trading position as soon as possible for the fear of being left-in on a current bad price direction.

78

A greedy trader would refrain selling a good position believing that the price will still ascend higher thus higher profits

A fearful trader would sell a position immediately believing that the price would already descend lower soon

A greedy trader is therefore eager to stay in a trading position greedy for more gains

81

While a fearful trader is therefore eager to sell to get out a trading position fearful of loses

82

A greedy trader is overwhelmed by the desire for more profits

A fearful trader is overwhelmed by the fear for lesser profits or loses

84

Greedy traders, becoming overly optimists, becomes a heavy buyers in the market

85

And fearful traders, becoming overly pessimists, becomes a heavy sellers in the market

Heavy buying often pushes the price higher

Heavy selling often pushes the price lower

88

Disaster happens to a greedy trader when he already entered and stayed in a trading position where the price had already reached the breaking point of the uptrend, and a reversal occurs leaving him in a buy high-sell low position;

Disaster happens to a fearful trader when he already exited or had avoided a trading position where the price had already reached the breaking point of the downtrend, and a reversal occurs leaving him a lost opportunity to buy low-sell high position.

A trader therefore should not be affected by
neither being too much greedy
nor being too much fearful

91

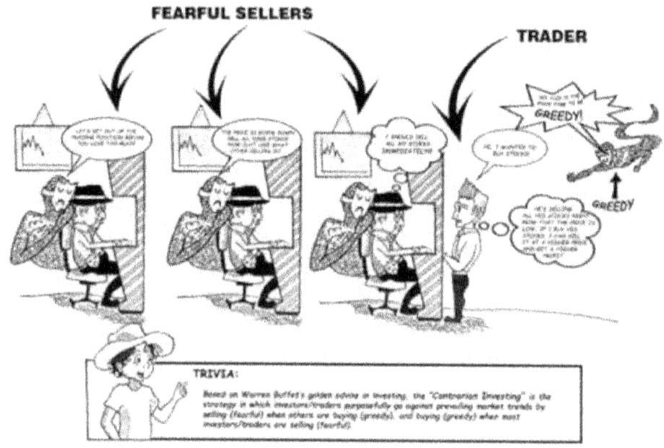

Thus it is said that a good trader only becomes greedy when others are fearful

And a good trader only becomes fearful when others a greedy.

It is because he only buys from the
pessimists and only sells to the optimists

94

Thus disasters are avoided!

95

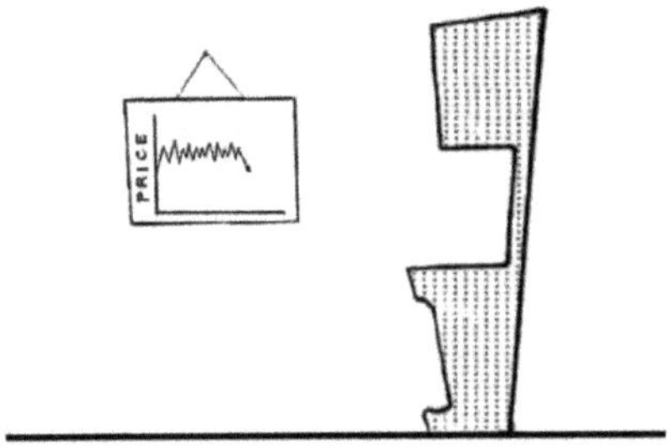

CHAPTER III:

The Price and the Market

Chapter III: The Price and The Market

Market and Price goes hand on hand

98

But nevertheless are different from one another

99

The market dictates the movement of the price

100

But it is the same price that moves the market to greed or fear

101

The market is rather not a place

102

But a group of people

103

The price is rather not a number

104

But a value based on one person's perception

105

A price maybe cheap to one

But it is the same price that is also expensive to the other

107

Thus, the measure of cheapness and expensiveness all depends on one's perception

108

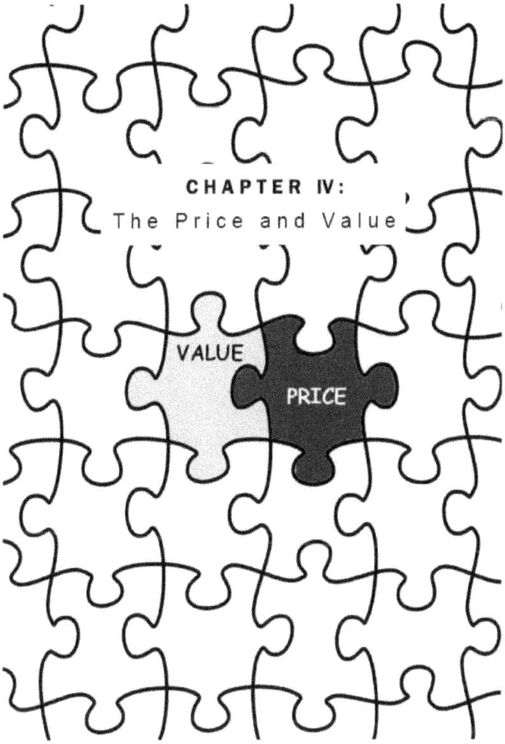
CHAPTER IV:
The Price and Value
VALUE
PRICE

Chapter IV: Price and Value

The value of a commodity, and the price of
a commodity are two different concepts

111

Value is intrinsic

112

Price is extrinsic

113

The intrinsic value is not
affected by the price

114

The price, however, is somehow affected by the market's perception

115

A commodity maybe of a lower value;
But the market will buy it at a higher price

A commodity maybe of a higher value;
But the market will sell it at a lower price

117

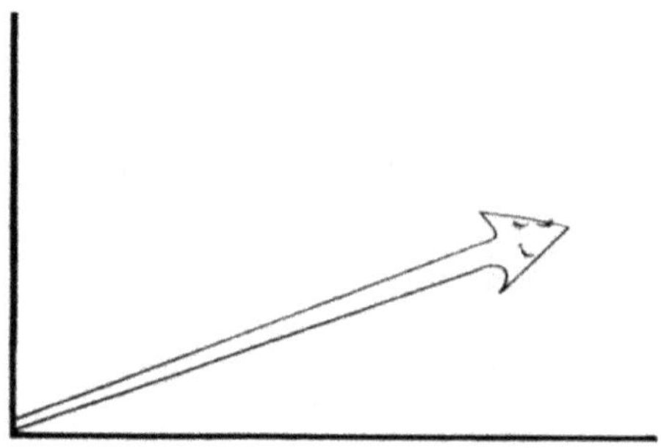

Value remains constant for a longer period

118

Price always change for a shorter period

119

TIPS

You can Buy when the Price is Lesser than its Value (Undervalued), then Sell when the Price is Greater than its Value (Overpriced)

A Good Trader understands the interplay between the Price and the Intrinsic Value

120

CHAPTER V:
The Stock Market

122

Chapter V: The Stock Market

Stock market is a sport

123

Where there are two teams
always competing

124

The Bulls

125

and the Bears

126

The other pushing the price up

127

The other pushing the price down

128

And everybody: investors, traders, hedge managers, institutional traders, stock brokerage firms, and insiders are players with different goals in mind and different strategies and approach

Different stocks are different battlefields to be played

130

Economic conditions, current news, rumours, etc forms the climate of the game

131

CHAPTER VI:

Nature of Demand and Market Price Fluctuations

133

Chapter VI: Nature of Demand and Market Price Fluctuations

The market price itself
represents the demand.

134

When the market price decreased and there is less or absence of demand in the market, Market price is more likely to be decrease more. (Continues Downtrend)

When the market price decreased,
and people began rushing to buy,
This is where the SUPPORT for demand enters.
(Support)

136

When the market price increased
and people still came rushing to buy,
Demand is still present. Market price
is thus more likely to increase more
(Continues Uptrend)

137

When the market price increased
and the people stopped buying but started selling,
this is where the RESISTANCE for Demand enters
(Resistance)

138

Full Text: The Tao of Trading

Chapter I: The Psychology of the Market

The Buyers and the Sellers

The market is composed of two opposite forces:
the buyers
and the sellers.

The buyers represent the demand,
The sellers represent the supply.

The Effect of Demand and Supply to Prices

It is said that:

When the demand is high, price tends to move up;

When the supply is high, price tends move down.

The Effect of Numbers of Buyers and Sellers to the Price

Therefore:

The more buyers over the sellers,
the more the price moves up;
The more the sellers over the buyers,
the more the price moves down.

The Different Trends

Price always follows three specific direction or trends:

Uptrend - Price can move up, when there are more buyers than the sellers;

Downtrend - Price can move down, when there are more sellers than the buyers;

No trend - Price moves sideways, when buyers and sellers both agree at a specific price range.

When Reversal Happens in Trends

Reversal usually happens in an uptrend, when there are already about no more buyers but sellers;
Reversal usually happens in a downtrend, when there are already about no more sellers but buyers.

The Buyer-Seller Cycle

Always remember that in a market, the buyers are potential sellers in the future.

A buyer will already become a seller once he already assumed that the price had reached a point that it is already high enough to close a trading position and gain profits.

A new buyer will come-in once he already assumed that the price had reached a point that it is already low enough to open a trading position which could in turn provide them profits in the future.

Different buyers had each different criteria when a specific price is low enough to open a trading position;

Different sellers had each different criteria when a specific price is high enough to close a trading position.

Support and Resistance

When majority of the buyers agree that the specific price point is low enough to open a trading position, this specific point becomes the "support";

When majority of the sellers agree that the specific price point is high enough to close a trading position, this specific point becomes the "resistance".

A specific point becomes the "support", when it blocks and supports the price from moving down lower;

A specific point becomes the "resistance", when it blocks and resists the price from moving up higher.

Thus the price bounces back once it hits the support and the resistance.

When the Support and Resistance Breaks

The price breaks the support when the sellers overcome the buyers and the majority of the buyers found a new lower price point that is cheaper enough to open a trading position;

The price breaks the resistance when the buyers overcome the sellers and the majority of the sellers found a new higher price point that is more expensive (and more profitable) enough to close a trading position.

When New Support and New Resistance is Created

A point of support, once broken, may become the new resistance;

A point of resistance, once broken, may become the new support.

Chapter II: The Trader

The Nature of a Trader

A trader is neither a buyer nor a seller.

But encompasses both being both a buyer and a seller.

Accumulators and Distributors

A person who only buys is not a trader,
but an accumulator unless he sells

A person who only sells is not a trader,
but a distributor unless he buys

Gamblers

A trader is a person who buy and sell for profit. Otherwise he is not a trader.

A person who carelessly buy and sell is not a trader, but a gambler.

When a Trader Buys and Sells

A good trader only buys when there is a good opportunity to buy,

A good trader only sells when there is a good opportunity to sell.

Two Sentiments in Trading

Thus created two divisions of trader in a market according to their sentiments:

A trader who wishes and hopes for the price to rise up further is a "Bull"

A trader who wishes and hopes for the price to go down further is a "Bear".

A bull is a predator that strikes its prey upwards

A bear is a predator that drags its prey downwards

The Bulls and the Bears

The Bulls are usually those who are waiting for the price to rise up until given an opportunity to sell at a higher price

The Bears are those who are waiting for the price to decline until given an opportunity to buy at a lower price

The Optimists and the Pessimists

Market situation creates two divisions of traders according to their attitude:

A trader becomes an optimist when he gives more value to a commodity than its actual value;
A trader becomes a pessimist when he gives lesser value to a commodity than its actual value.

Thus, a good trader takes profits through buying from a pessimist and selling to the optimist.

Two Dangerous Emotions in Trading

A good trader always keep himself in check from being vulnerable to two dangerous emotions in trading:
one is when he is greedy;

the other one is when he is fearful.

Emotions clouds the judgment of a trader:
A trader may overestimate too much a commodity when he is greedy;

A trader may underestimate too much a commodity when he is fearful.

The Psychology of Greed and Fear

A greedy trader who buys would therefore pay even at a higher price believing that the price would even ascend higher soon;
A fearful trader who buys would therefore not pay even at a lower price believing that the price would even descend lower soon.

A greedy trader is therefore eager to buy to get in a trading position

While a fearful trader is therefore eager to sell to get out a trading position

A greedy trader is overwhelmed by the desire of entering or staying in a trading position as soon as possible for the fear of being left-out on a current good price direction;

A fearful trader is overwhelmed by the desire of exiting or staying out of a trading position as soon as possible for the fear of being left-in on a current bad price direction.

A greedy trader would refrain selling a good position believing that the price will still ascend higher thus higher profits;
A fearful trader would sell a position immediately believing that the price would already descend lower soon.

A greedy trader is therefore eager to stay in a trading position greedy for more gains
While a fearful trader is therefore eager to sell to get out a trading position fearful of loses

A greedy trader is overwhelmed by the desire for more profits;

A fearful trader is overwhelmed by the fear for lesser profits or loses.

Heavy Buying and Heavy Selling

Greedy traders, becoming overly optimists, becomes a heavy buyers in the market;
And fearful traders, becoming overly pessimists, becomes a heavy sellers in the market.

Heavy buying often pushes the price higher.
Heavy selling often pushes the price lower.

Disasters in Trading

Disaster happens to a greedy trader when he already entered and stayed in a trading position where the price had already reached the breaking point of the uptrend, and a reversal occurs leaving him in a buy high-sell low position;
Disaster happens to a fearful trader when he already exited or had avoided a trading position where the price had already reached the breaking point of the downtrend, and a reversal occurs leaving him a lost opportunity to buy low-sell high position.

A trader therefore should not be affected by neither being too much greedy nor being too much fearful.

Contrarian Trading Strategy

Thus it is said that a good trader only becomes greedy
when others are fearful;
And a good trader only becomes fearful when others a greedy.

It is because he only buys from the pessimists and only sells to the optimists.

Thus disasters are avoided

Chapter III: The Price and the Market

Market and Price goes hand on hand;

But nevertheless different from one another.

The market dictates the movement of the price.
But it is the same price that moves the market to greed or fear.

The market is rather not a place,

But a group of people.

The price is rather not a number

But a value based on one person's perception.

A price maybe cheap to one,

But it is the same price that is also expensive to the other.

Thus, the measure of cheapness and expensiveness all depends on one's perception

Chapter IV: The Price and Value

The value of a commodity, and the price of a commodity are two different concept.
Value is intrinsic
Price is extrinsic

The intrinsic value is not affected by the price
The price, however, is somehow affected by the market's perception:

A commodity maybe of a lower value;
But the market will buy it at a higher price
A commodity maybe of a higher value;
But the market will sell it at a lower price

Value remains constant for a longer period
Price always change for a shorter period

A Good Trader understands the interplay between the Price and the Intrinsic Value

Chapter V: The Stock Market

Stock market is a sport

Where there are two teams always competing:
The Bulls
and the Bears:

The other pushing the price up

The other pushing the price down

And everybody: investors, traders, hedge managers, institutional traders, stock brokerage firms, and insiders are players with different goals in mind and different strategies and approach

Different stocks are different battlefields to be played.

Economic conditions, current news, rumours, etc forms the climate of the game

Chapter VI: Nature of Demand and Market Price Fluctuations

The market price itself represents the demand.

When the market price decreased and there is less or absence of demand in the market. Market price is more likely to be decrease more. (Continues Downtrend)

When the market price decreased, and people began rushing to buy. This is where the SUPPORT for demand enters. (Support)

When the market price increased and people still came rushing to buy, Demand is still present. Market price is thus more likely to increase more (Continues Uptrend)

When the market price increased and the people stopped buying but started selling, this is where the RESISTANCE for Demand enters (Resistance)

About the Author

J.M. Benavidez Estoque is a graduate of BS Psychology with Latin Honors in St. Joseph's College of Quezon City. He also finished his Diploma in Industrial Relations in the University of the Philippines - Diliman. He had worked as a Part-Time Professor in Statistics and in Experimental Psychology and is currently working in the Government.

His earnings as Trader in the Stock Market during his active years helped him save for his further education. He is currently studying Bachelor of Law in Manuel L. Quezon University as of this writing.

Connect with the Author:

Facebook:

https://www.facebook.com/johnmarc.estoque/

Facebook Page:

https://www.facebook.com/PhilippineSocialConservativeMovement

Goodreads:

https://www.goodreads.com/author/show/6603867.J_M_Benavidez_Estoque

Amazon:

amazon.com/author/jmestoque

Other Books by the Author

On Legal Profession: A Philosophical Discussion from Plato to Rousseau

125 Reflections of Marcus Aurelius: A Topical Index to the Meditations

The Conservative Wisdom of Confucius: A Topical Index to the Analects

An Introduction to the Treatise on Law by St. Thomas Aquinas

About the Illustrator

Lyndon Regalario is a graduate of BS Architecture in Technological University of the Philippines-Manila. Aside from being an illustrator, he is also a former apprentice in different design firms and still pursues his career in architecture. His favorite medium is watercolor on paper, wherein he creates his illustration by means of traditional techniques. His love for drawing since he was young brought him into different drawing competitions on his early age; and also a cartoonist of their school newspaper during his grade school and high school years.

www.ingramcontent.com/pod-product-compliance
Lightning Source LLC
Chambersburg PA
CBHW050527240926
51846CB00003B/722
* 9 7 8 6 2 1 4 1 9 1 0 3 1 *